Crocus Candles

On the bank beneath the hedge, and along the
garden edge—coloured candles are ablaze—
making bright the wintry days.
Fairy flames of bloom we see—shining under
bush and tree—Ivory and mauve and gold,
bringing warmth to hearts grown cold.
Where these little candles burn—griefs recede
and hopes return. Crocuses from God are
sent—to illume the gates of Lent.

Quietude

Too much noise and too much hurry—too much talk and too much worry.
. . . Entertainment!
Wordly pleasure! Not enough of peace and leisure. We are nervous and distraught. Oh for rest and quiet thought! Time in which to dream awhile—fleeing from the false and vile . . . From the sordid and the crude. In our hours of quietude—we escape, and

breathe the air—of the pure, the clean, the fair.
Evil is before our eyes—yet if we are truly wise—we shall cling to an Ideal—to the perfect and the real.
. . . Vice and virtue; this is Life. Shame and glory, Peace and strife . . . We must learn with heart and will—to be silent, to be still; every worthless thought subdued—in the bliss of quietude.

The Light at the Back of the Cloud

At the back of the cloud there's a splendour—in the regions beyond human sight. Though the sky may look stormy remember—that it veils the unchangeable light.

At the back of the cloud there's a lining—and it's golden and silver and blue—for the brightness of heaven is shining—on the side that is hidden from you.

When adversity comes, never mind it. Face the storm with your shoulders unbowed. And remember that God is behind it—in the light at the back of the cloud.

Make a Rainbow

If your world looks gloomy and you're feeling grim and glum. Make a rainbow for yourself, don't wait for one to come. Don't sit watching at the window for the clouds to part. There'll soon be a rainbow if you start one in your heart.

Take some lovely thought out of a poem or a prayer. Turn it over in your mind and let it linger there. Keep out every memory that dims the light within—and hold on to the magic word that lets the brightness in.

Work your own small miracle and make the dull days glow. Put some sunshine into life and let the glory show. Make a rainbow for yourself with colours brave and gay—And underneath its golden arch your cares will fade away.

Faith Can See

When you look out at your garden on a wintry day—you see it in its death-like sleep, all desolate and grey . . . It's hard to think that just below that frosted counterpane—all the flowers are waiting to come up and out again.

It strains the imagination to believe that they are there. The earth looks cold and lifeless and the trees are stark and bare. The mind says, "No, it cannot be," but faith says, "It is so." For faith can see the hidden glory underneath the snow.

Sometimes when you look out at the world your heart despairs. It is hard to think there is a God who really cares—but just as faith can see the spring beneath the winter's pall—Faith can see a Father's loving kindness over all.

Best Side Out

Turn your troubles inside out, and maybe you will find—something good; for like the clouds, they're often silver-lined . . . Have you got a problem? Don't despair with tears and sighs. Someday it may prove to be a blessing in disguise.
Have you got a sorrow or a secret tragedy? Do not lose your faith. Time will enable you to see—the guidance and the sure protection of an unseen hand. Dare we doubt Him in the things we do not understand?
Life is double-sided; there's a wrong side and a right; a sad side and a happy side; a black side and a bright.
. . . So if things look dark to you just change your thoughts about. Life will look quite different if you turn it best side out.

Golden Windows

When the Sun is sinking in a blaze of crimson light—the street is full of golden windows, radiant and bright . . . The windows looking to the west that catch the fiery gleams—like golden windows opening on the landscape of our dreams.
The mind has golden windows . . . golden thoughts from which we see—the shining vistas stretching out into Eternity . . . Windows of the Soul at which we

stand with hungry eyes—and strive to read the
message of God's writing in the skies.
Windows of our Memories that open on the Past—
sometimes golden-tinted—or with shadows overcast
. . . Then there are the windows of our Faith from
which we lean—and gaze enthralled beyond the
world to a diviner scene.

Treasures of Darkness

There are treasures to be found in places desolate. Hidden gold in secret mines. Things fine and true and great—are often born of bitterness of pain and poverty. Many a lovely thing was fashioned by adversity.

If we dwelt like heavenly beings in perpetual light—We should never see the glory of the starry night . . . If Joy were our companion all along a broad bright way—we should dance our way through life forgetting how to pray.

Rise and Shine

If you want to look your best, to flourish and to thrive—if you want to have good health, to live and stay alive—Remember that your outlook has a lot to do with it. Happy thoughts will tend to keep you young and make you fit.

Give the day a sparkle, full of cheerfulness and hope. Whatever looms ahead refuse to grumble or to mope. Make a pleasure of your work, enjoying what you do. It can be a bore or fun. It all depends on you.

In your mind, you have the power to choose what you will be. You can change yourself, your world, your personality. Every day you get the chance to take a different line. You can sink or, like a fountain, you can rise and shine.

Into the Light

As I watched the sunlight trailing gold across the floor—I became aware of Someone at my heart's closed door—like an angel visitor from somewhere far away—with a secret message of good tidings to convey.

The door had long been locked and barred for I had suffered much. The heavy bolts had rusted, but they yielded to my touch. I opened wide the creaking door and found that it was Spring; I felt the sun upon my face. I heard a blackbird sing.

I saw the damson trees in bloom. I saw the lilac hedge. I saw a spray of honeysuckle at the windowledge . . . In that moment I regained my spiritual sight—and with a prayer of thankfulness stepped out into the light.

Beyond the Shadows

Sunshine beyond the shadows—
Dawning beyond the night;
Springtime beyond the Winter—
colour and warmth and light.

Gladness beyond the sorrow—
Laughter beyond the tears . . .
Hope like a star at evening—
glowing beyond the fears.

Courage! Beyond the morrow—
you will find peace again . . .
Strength and Desire returning—
Rapture beyond the pain.

Somewhere beyond the shadows—
there's a new life for you—
Lift up your eyes, believing—
and it will all come true.

The Trail

Leave a trail of happiness as you go along—Make a bit of sunshine as you pass; try to leave upon the air the echo of your song—sowing seeds of friendship in the grass.

Build your little wayside shrines upon Life's winding road—Someone coming after you may find . . . Courage, hope and strength with which to bear a heavy load—On the trail that you have left behind.

Try to leave each place a little brighter when you go. Many times you'll falter and you'll fail . . . But who can tell what lovely things will grow—from the seeds you plant along the trail.

Before the Sun goes Down

One by one we tear the leaves from off the almanac. The weeks rush by, the months slip past. We cannot call them back—but we can get the best and brightest from the present day. Do not let the precious sands of time just run away.

Gather up the gold they leave and with a grateful thought—count up all the mercies that the passing hours have brought . . . No matter how a day may make you fume and fret and frown—Wrest a blessing out of it before the sun goes down.

Glimpses

Life's made up of hints and glimpses—As we're passing by—here a gleam and there a glimmer flash before the eye . . . We cannot view the whole of it—but as we go our way, we see a flower amongst the weeds, and gold beyond the grey.

A word passed with a stranger. An encounter. Just a glance—into someone else's life . . . a picture seen by chance . . . A peep into Love's mystery . . . a glimpse and nothing more—Like some quiet and lovely place seen through an open door.

We are in a hurry and we have no time to spare—to wander and to wonder at the beauty everywhere . . . We cannot see the length and breadth of earth and sea and sky—We must be content with glimpses—as we're passing by.

Far Away

The days grow shorter as the year rolls towards its end. Too soon it seems the light grows fainter and the nights descend. Brief the journey of the sun. December days are drear—but they bring us to the morning of another year.

At this point upon the road the heart is strangely stirred—for far away we hear the singing of an April bird . . . with brighter hope and lighter step we tread the wintry hills—having caught upon the wind the breath of daffodils.

Happy Morning

Greet the day with happy heart and vow that it will be—a well-lived and a worthwhile day. Accept it gratefully—as a good and precious gift, a newly given chance—to wrest a blessing out of every twist of circumstance.

Grey the day may look to you when first you wake to it. Don't go by appearance. Later on it may be lit—with sunny gleams and golden dreams, adventure and romance. You must not judge a day by what it looks like at a glance.

Even though the day holds out no hope of happiness. Don't despise it or despair for you can never guess—what it may unfold before the sunset dies away. Greet with glad thanksgiving the beginning of each day.

Our Needs

Our needs are few and simple—we who seek Life's sweetest joy—in homely things; the little pleasures that can never cloy. These are our needs . . . a cosy room—a chair beside the fire; a well-loved book—a quiet hour—What more could we desire?
A window that reveals a bit of green—some grass—a tree; plain food—eggs, fruit, a crusty loaf, fresh milk—a cup of tea; warm clothes; stout shoes for rainy days—clean linen in the store; a bed for rest when work is done. No man dare ask for more.
Lord, grant the day is coming when the poorest man and wife—possess the secret riches of the happiness of Life . . . This is the hidden treasure sought by peasants and by kings—the power to find contentment in the joy of simple things.